Shaking
Like a
Leaf

A Triumphant Story of
Overcoming Anxiety

Dina Comer

ISBN 978-1-0980-7907-9 (paperback)
ISBN 978-1-0980-7908-6 (digital)

Christian Faith Publishing, Inc.
832 Park Avenue
Meadville, PA 16335
www.christianfaithpublishing.com

Printed in the United States of America

Introduction

Paul tells us in one of his letters to the Corinthians:

> We have this treasure in jars of clay to show that this all-surpassing power is from God and not from us. We are hard-pressed on every side but NOT crushed; perplexed, but NOT in despair; persecuted, but NOT abandoned; struck down, but NOT destroyed. (2 Corinthians 4:7–9 NIV)

Those words from Paul are incredibly comforting especially for those of us who have felt hard-pressed on every side and struck down, thinking we might be destroyed. Paul is reminding Christ's followers that we have an incredible treasure inside our very own bodies. Our flesh or "jar of clay," as he puts it, signifies something ordinary and simple on the outside with something of incredible value on the inside. It has taken me a long time to truly understand this scripture. Fortunately though, when I got it, I got it!

There have definitely been incredibly scary days in my life when I have felt hard-pressed on every side, perplexed and struck down. It was in the thick of those days when I learned how to hold on to the treasure of Jesus Christ on the inside of me and realized I was really not crushed. I did not have to give into despair. As I wrestled with my heart, mind, and emotions, I discovered an incredible truth in a very personal way. Simply put, this once weak and feeble vessel was not abandoned. My God was with me.

For so long, I had moments when I was overwhelmed because my heart was saying one thing, and my mind was screaming another. It was as if every toxic emotion seemed to be making its way through my blood stream. Every fear came screaming in my ear as I tried to remember the promises that I am to live by. Despair does not belong to me. For every single fear or uncertainty that I face, there is an empty grave reminding me of the greatest victory of all time. It's just that some days it was—is—easier to say than to truly believe and live by especially under a severe attack.

To count how many times I have felt struck down by the enemy of my soul to the point where I thought I was going crazy would be fruitless. Rather, I choose to count the number of times when I have been reminded of the powerful promises found in God's word and just how precious I am to the One who calls me by name. Because of that, I have learned how to overcome.

Call it friend or foe, I know the reality of severe panic and fear and pain. I've been acquainted with them more than I care to admit—like an uninvited guest that keeps popping up in your life when you least expect it. When you're in a room full of people, and everyone around you seems to be feeling normal except you, on the outside you look fine. But there are things going on inside your mind and body that make you want to scream or, in the least, go run and hide. When you can hardly catch your breath, when your heart is racing so wildly fast, your stomach is churning. Your brain won't shut off. The fear will not release its grip on you. When you're convinced your life is at its end, and no one can seem to understand why. It's when you are shaking like a leaf that the Prince of Peace can show you who He truly is!

Mayhem at the Celebration Station

I t was not the sunniest of days but certainly nice enough to venture out to the Celebration Station with our good friends who were visiting from Florida. My husband and I and our two young children had only moved to Tennessee from Florida eight months prior to this day. My friend, Cheryl, and her husband, Troy, along with their two little children, had been in town a couple days when we all decided to take our kids out for some fun on this spring day near Knoxville.

None of us had ever been to the Celebration Station before. It was quite the festive place for young families to go with their children. There was plenty to do indoors and outdoors. Since all of our children were under the age of five, we decided to all stick together, explore all the fun things to do, and play a round of Putt-Putt golf outside.

Our kids were having a blast together playing with their little plastic golf clubs. It must have been an adorable site with all of the laughter and giggles surrounding our two families—at least enough so that the two young men from the "Knoxville News" were drawn to us.

The older of the two gentlemen was the one that spoke. He walked up and kindly introduced himself and his assistant to our two families and explained the reason that they approached us. He handed us his business card as he explained that the city's newspaper would be doing an article on families having fun together, and we seemed like the perfect families to interview. Obviously, we felt honored. The gentleman had taken a few snapshots of us then began to ask a range of family-focused questions. Most of the questions were directed to my husband and I.

The "interview" certainly did not seem to last very long. The gentleman thanked us kindly for allowing him to take up some of our time and then began to walk way.

It only took two seconds for me to realize that something was very wrong. Then it hit me. Once I turned back around, Hannah, our two-year-old toddler, was nowhere in sight. I began to call her name as did my husband and our friends who I assumed knew where she was. Once many long seconds went by and none of us had her in our sight, it dawned on me. This could have been a scam!

The assistant to our "newspaper" gentleman was already nowhere in sight, but the man who had approached us was. I ran as fast as I could, and very much unlike my normal behavior, I grabbed this man by the shirt, turned him around and screamed, "Where is my baby? What did you men do with my baby?"

I'm not sure how many more times I asked those same questions, but I do know he adamantly assured me they didn't have my baby. I saw from my peripheral vision that my husband was already running toward the parking lot of the Celebration Station, knowing that he would jump in front of any car that might be trying to leave that parking lot with our baby girl.

Panic began to set in at a whole new level as the seconds and minutes went by. My mind was reeling as my husband and friends were searching for Hannah while keeping a hold of the other three children. My eyes spotted the pond that was in the very center of the park close to where we had been playing Putt-Putt. Perhaps she fell in there, and we didn't notice.

As my mind was reeling, the only thing I could think to do was jump in. And that's exactly what I did. I went back and forth swooshing my arms through the pond to see if I could feel her, all the while loudly crying out to God—more like screaming—to save her. I kept screaming over and over, "In the name of Jesus, she will live and not die!" I was feeling overwhelmed and in an absolute panic. I didn't know if she had fallen in this water or if someone had taken her.

In between my crying out to God, I would look around at the hundreds of people meandering around the park and screamed over to them, "Somebody find my baby!" All of a sudden, one by one, men began jumping in the pond with me, helping me search for my baby girl. It felt like an unreal scene from a movie, but it was my reality in that moment. By this time, I saw workers from the Celebration Station talking on walkie-talkies and shutting down all the different rides around the park. It was as if all time had stopped, and everything was happening in slow motion. The only thing that wasn't slow was my heart. It was beating at a rate that was beyond what I felt it could handle.

There was a woman who was yelling at me from the side of the pond, and finally, she got my attention. She was yelling for me to come to her. I don't remember much of what she was saying, but I do remember when I got close to her, she put her hands on my shoulders and made me look her in the eyes. She kept asking me over and over, "What does she look like? What does your little girl look like?" I stood there numb like I couldn't even describe my daughter. All I eventually blurted out was, "Blue overalls, blue overalls!"

I had dressed Hannah in little blue Osh Kosh overalls that day. The woman let go of my shoulders and ran away in a fury. I continued in the pond as my husband returned empty-handed and jumped in the pond with the rest of us, assuming we knew something he didn't. It certainly seemed like an eternity had passed, but then I heard her—that woman. She was yelling at me again. Above the noise, above the crowd, above the panic, I heard that woman ask me, "Is this her?" I remember my husband and I looking that way as the woman began to lift up a little girl above the crowd—our little girl.

She was standing in a gated area of the park that seemed so far away, but she was close enough that we could see it was our Hannah. To say we ran to her would be an understatement. In that moment, it seemed again like all time stood still. I vaguely remember hearing claps all around the park. Then I didn't know if I should laugh or cry—although I was doing both. I struggled between being embarrassed by the mayhem we had caused but feeling overwhelmed and greatly relieved beyond words that our baby girl had been found alive.

To this day, we have no idea exactly what happened to our little girl or how she got away from us unnoticed with four responsible parents hovering over our children—even in the midst of that so-called interview. Oddly enough, we never got the photographs we had been promised by the gentleman from the "Knoxville News" who said he'd mail them to us, nor did we ever see a family-fun article come out. In fact, when we called that newspaper inquiring about that situation, there was no such story being worked on. One thing was for certain, I would never, ever want to go back to the Celebration Station again, and I would not want to offer my family for a random newspaper article ever again either.

Six Months Later

I was in the hallway bathroom putting on some makeup while my
kids were in the nearby living room watching Dumbo. Joshua,
our five-year-old son, was sitting on the floor in front of the TV,
playing with some of his toys while his little sister, now three, sat in
the recliner, cuddled up with her favorite blanket, watching this fam-
ily-favorite movie. Ever so casually, as a five-year-old would do, my
son came over to me and said, "Mommy, Hannah's acting funny!"
Of course, my assumption was that she had climbed down from her
chair and was perhaps dancing along with a song from the movie. I
peeked around the wall, using a sweet voice, I asked Hannah if she
was being silly. I was already smiling, assuming I would see her dancing away by the TV. To my shock, that was not what I saw. Instead,
I saw my little girl laying facedown on the wooden floor, making a
funny sound indeed.

As I ran over to my daughter, I picked her up, called out her
name, and asked her if she had fallen. But she wasn't responding.
She felt like a rag doll in my arms as I lifted her, unable to hold
her head up or hold onto me with her own strength. She was making gurgling sounds, but then they were more like gasps, one after
another. Her eyes wouldn't—couldn't—even focus on me. Instead,
they were glazed over, looking in a different direction. It was as if
she was lifeless, yet she was still breathing even though they were
very short breaths. I kept telling her to "look at Mommy!" But she
couldn't do it. Her eyes were rolling in the back of her head. I asked
her, her name, but she was totally nonresponsive. Panic set in. I ran
to the kitchen. She was still in my arms. I called 911 and did the

best I could to keep my emotions in check while talking to the 911 operator as the ambulance made its way to our house.

Minutes went by and then the emergency workers arrived. They immediately took my little girl out of my arms and laid her on the kitchen table. They mentioned something about the possibility of cutting her throat open with some instrument if they found her airway was blocked by something. They were asking questions, and I was doing my best to keep focused and answer. Within moments, the decision was made that they would need to transport her to the local hospital. A neighbor was going to watch my son. My husband was on his way home from work to meet me at the hospital.

I had never heard of a febrile seizure before. After some tests were run and after a neurosurgeon saw her, that's what we were told. Our daughter had experienced a febrile seizure. They explained that it is a seizure caused when a child has a fever that comes on very suddenly. They then explained the reason she wasn't responding normally yet was because after a febrile seizure, the brain has to *reset* (along the lines of a computer rebooting). Needless to say, it was a very scary experience and one I never wanted to repeat. However, the doctor did share that it was very likely she could have one again since they usually repeat themselves in children between the ages of three and five.

It had now been about five months since that scary experience of Hannah having a seizure. I was sitting at my computer, working on something, while my husband was downstairs in our basement. The children had been playing in their playroom when Hannah walked in. She came in and said with her little sweet voice, "Mommy, hold me." I picked her up to sit her in my lap, asking her what was the matter because I could tell something was wrong. Before she could even begin to answer, her eyes rolled in the back of her head, her little body began to shake, her lips began to quiver, then turned blue, and she began to foam at the mouth. I screamed for my husband who came running up the stairs. My mind was racing as once again panic set in. My husband took her into his arms, and I ran to the phone to call 911. Hannah was experiencing another febrile seizure. I hadn't seen the first one. This one happened in my arms.

As horrible as this was, fortunately, we were blessed to have an amazing pediatrician who thoroughly calmed our deepest fears and shared with us some simple things we could do if this would happen again, as well as explained some things to do to help prevent them. Thankfully, that was the last febrile seizure she ever had.

Rewind: A Little Backstory

I had made the decision to be a court reporter when I was in middle school. I kept that goal in mind through my teen years and went through high school knowing exactly what I wanted to do once I graduated. Business school was hard work, but I accomplished my goal and received my specialized court reporting degree before the age of twenty. I graduated from college within a few weeks of getting married, and my future looked bright. I was ready for this brand-new adventure of being a wife and career woman to begin.

My husband and I built our first house shortly after our first anniversary while I was working as a freelance court reporter. After three years of marriage, we started to add to our family. First, our precious son, Joshua, came along> And then two and a half years later, our little girl, Hannah, came along. We felt quite content, at least for the most part. We loved our little family. We were very involved with our home church, and we had family and many great friends close by.

My husband had a dream that he had been holding onto for many years. At one point in time, athletics had been his passion, playing football from Pee Wee League to college football. But this was a different dream outside of the athletic arena. He was (still is) a great musician, singer, and songwriter, and he had a dream to pursue a music career. Even though he had a good job where we were living, and we were very involved with our church (he was the worship leader there on staff), his passion for music and the desire to be in a Christian band was still burning in his heart.

Some friends from his college had contacted him, and they were ready to start a band together. This was something they had talked about years earlier. The only problem was they all lived in Tennessee (where he had gone to college), and we lived in Florida. After months of discussion and serious prayer, we made the big decision to move. It was definitely a big deal for me because I would be leaving my home town, my family, my friends, my church, literally everything I had ever known. However, I knew it was something I needed to do for my husband. I wanted him to be able to pursue his dream.

We sold our house quicker than expected, and we found and bought a beautiful country home in Tennessee. My husband got the very first job he applied for there. All the pieces easily fell right into place. We were ready to start a new adventure in Tennessee. After taking a few months to get settled in and while my husband was working hard at his office job and pursuing his music dream, I decided that I was ready to take a leap of faith and start my own court reporting business in my new town. It was something that I had always said I would do one day.

To say that it was easy to launch my own business in Tennessee would be an understatement. The first phone call I made to a local attorney landed me an interview. Once I met with him and shared with him what I wanted to do, I was in. My new court reporting business took off, and I had more business than I had ever imagined. My husband was working full time. His band was beginning to record and do concerts. And I was keeping on my toes, doing my best to be a great wife, a wonderful mother, and a successful career woman. So far, so good.

Sure, there were some trying times along the way—still dealing with the separation from all my family and friends back in Florida and getting used to being states away from everything and everyone I had ever known. Of course, the crazy ordeal with our baby girl at the Celebration Station was no help, and learning about febrile seizures in a very up close and personal way felt like an unwanted guest in my life. But at the end of each day, I still considered my life so blessed that I felt like I could conquer the world.

Full Steam Ahead

We had been in Tennessee for close to two years now, and my life was running full steam ahead. In the normalcy of life, things seemed to be flowing decently with our family life and schedules. Then without any notice, another uninvited guest arrived.

It was in the middle of the day, in the middle of the week, and I was at my computer working on a deposition transcript for an upcoming court case. My son was at a nearby church preschool program, and my daughter was happily playing with her toys right beside me on the floor. When out of nowhere, it happened. In that moment, I wasn't exactly sure what *it* was, but *it* was happening to me.

I cannot put into words the feeling or sensation that I felt in my body. My heart began to race at such a fast pace, I thought it was going to explode. I am almost sure I could even hear it beating out of my chest. I was having a heart attack, or rather I thought I was.

I didn't know of anyone in my family who had ever had a heart attack before. But as the seconds passed, my heart continued to race, and I became convinced that that's what was happening. I felt like I was losing my ability to breathe at a normal pace. I thought I was going to panic, and that I would certainly pass out. I couldn't understand what was happening to me in those moments or why.

I considered myself a pretty healthy eater, and I had not been sick in any way. For the most part, I was in good shape. I even led an aerobics class a couple times a week at a local church in town. Was I really having a heart attack right here, right now, at the age of twenty-seven with my little girl playing with her dolls down by my feet?

My heart continued to race for a little bit longer, then another feeling began to have my focus. My whole body began to tremble, and I felt totally weird. No fancy word for it. I just felt weird. Something was wrong. That's when the panic really began to settle in. The fear that began to take over was almost paralyzing.

All I could think to do was call the home-schooled sisters who were our babysitters that lived nearby. I frantically shared that something was wrong with me—that I thought I was having a heart attack—and could at least one of them come over immediately. I knew something serious was happening to me, and I didn't want my baby girl to be alone if I lost consciousness. I was trying to figure out what I needed to do. Did I have to call my husband? Did I have to call 911? Did I just need to lie down for a few minutes until this passed? My husband's office was about fifty minutes away. So even if I did call him, I wasn't sure if I could hold on long enough for him to get home.

By the time my husband did get home, everything was fine. At least it was fine in the sense of what I had gone through about fifty minutes ago. I almost felt embarrassed or silly as I was explaining to him what exactly had happened to me. I could only imagine what he was thinking, because the more I talked about it, the crazier it sounded to me. My heart was now back to beating at a normal rhythm, and the weird feeling I had earlier was totally gone.

There was no doubt that something had happened. I knew what I had felt, but since my husband was now home, and the rest of the night was moving on as usual, I decided to chalk it up to an odd situation. The next many days went by, and life was back to normal. So it was easy to just assume all was well.

It was another Friday night, and we had just put the kids to bed. My husband and I had just settled down on the couch for the evening to watch a movie. We had only been sitting on the couch for a few minutes when it happened. All of a sudden, in the comfort of my living room, relaxed in my pj's and enjoying my husband's company, my heart began to race again out of control. It was as if it came on out of nowhere.

My heart was racing at such a high rate, I was convinced that not only could my husband feel it, he could hear it too. *It* was back! That same weird feeling that I had recently experienced came over me again. My mind, once again, became paralyzed with fear that I was about to die. Something was definitely wrong. This was no joke! Just like the first time, the whole episode lasted for several long minutes. With my heart racing, my mind gripped with fear, all while my body was shaking uncontrollably. Those several minutes seemed to have lasted for hours.

Immediately after everything in my body settled back to normal, my husband insisted that I make the first appointment that I could get with a doctor. I hadn't gotten established in Tennessee with a doctor yet simply because I had never needed to up until that time. So I made the first appointment I could get.

I explained everything that had happened on those two occasions to the new doctor. He was a kind, older man. I remember him sharing with me, as a father would say to his daughter, that I was way too young for a heart attack. Sitting in that examination room, he convinced me that I did not have a heart attack, nor was I on the verge of one.

Blood work was ordered, and the blood work came back. It was all normal. In my follow-up visit, he shared that I seemed in good enough health and that I should not be concerned about anything serious. That seemed to satisfy me, at least while he was sharing those words with me right there in his office. I decided in that moment just to chalk those two occasions up to awkward situations. However, deep down inside, I think I knew better.

On and On, It Goes

Weeks would go by, and life took on its normal routine once again. After a while though, when I would least expect it, *it* would happen again. Unfortunately, I still didn't know what *it* was. I truly had no clue what was happening to me. Just when I thought I was doing fine going about a normal day, I would find myself having a difficult time simply breathing in a regular rhythm. I would have to take a few extra deep breaths just to really catch my breath. Then out of nowhere, my heart would suddenly begin to race. And along with all the crazy things I would feel, fear would paralyze me in a very tangible way.

All I knew to do in those moments was to go find a place to lay down and battle through that crazy episode as my entire body would shake uncontrollably. No doubt, I sounded like a broken record because all I could say over and over was *Jesus! Jesus! Jesus!* while one of my episodes were happening. Then when it would pass, I continued on as normal as possible, trying to find a clue as to what was triggering me.

With each passing episode, I was becoming more and more frustrated because I wanted to understand what my body was doing. What was happening to me? For the life of me, I could not figure this out.

I continued to pray and cry out to the Lord every single time it would happen. I kept asking God to show me what was wrong, to heal me, and to give me understanding. Up to this time, I had no idea of the spiritual, emotional, and physical battle I was really headed into. I also had no clue how long this battle would take for me to get through. I just knew my life was all beginning to unravel.

It was suggested that I may have a heart condition called mitral valve prolapse. So as requested, I had heart monitoring tests done. The good news was I didn't have mitral valve prolapse. In fact, my heart showed no signs of anything being wrong with it, although I was convinced it had to be something with my heart because of the pace that it would race during these scary, sporadic episodes. Still I was left wondering what was going on with my body. No one had the answers yet to my questions.

These episodes had no respect of time. I could be driving down the road, doing dishes in my kitchen, sitting on my couch, giving my kids a bath—you name it—and they would just come out of nowhere when I least expected it, totally unannounced and unwarranted from my perspective. *It* kept happening. Days would go by, sometimes even weeks. I would be just fine. Then with no warning and nothing to trigger it, my heart would begin to race, my body would feel totally bizarre, fear would grip me, my mind would become paralyzed, and I would feel as if I was physically and emotionally having a meltdown wherever I was.

A Praying Woman Indeed

Let me assure you, I was a praying woman. I was a Christian who was solid in my faith and passionate about serving the Lord. I had given my life to the Lord shortly before my sixteenth birthday after spending the first many years of my life not having a clue about the Lord at all. Once I did surrender my life to him, I began going to church, growing in my faith and learning what it meant to truly follow Jesus passionately and wholeheartedly with my life. But here I was, over a decade later, and I was being tested in my faith like never before.

Every time *it* would happen, I would cry out to God with whatever strength and fervency I had in that moment. I knew how to pray, and I believed in God's healing power. I was certain God was able to heal me.

My husband was a great prayer partner and quite the trooper during this horrific season. When I would experience one of these episodes, he would pray with me, over me, for me, constantly calming my greatest fears. He would pray with great authority, but I knew he was concerned about me because we had no definitive answers to what was happening to me. And being the man that he is, he was frustrated because he couldn't fix it.

Unfortunately, these paralyzing no-name episodes kept coming, and coming, and coming. At no specific time, for no specific reason, they would come when I would least expect it. When I felt good, I felt good. I could go days without anything happening. And every time I would have a break from these attacks, I would convince myself once again that I was just fine. That was, of course, until it would happen again.

For obvious reasons, I could not pretend that nothing was happening to me. I was beginning to realize that I really was in the greatest spiritual warfare of my life, but I also desperately needed some practical answers to explain what this was or why this was happening. There had to be a name for it.

Finally, after many months of battling through these episodes of my heart racing uncontrollably, with shortness of breath, my body going numb, and shaking like a leaf in a wild storm (not to mention that overall weird feeling that I couldn't quite put into words), I simply didn't know what else to do. I decided to find a female doctor—an ob-gyn—for a checkup. Maybe something in *that* part of my body might give a clue.

She Called It by Name

She was the first doctor who actually did a personal sit-down consultation before she began my first examination. I was about ten minutes into the consultation. I had been answering her questions, and I had shared about moving our little family from my home state of Florida, starting our new life in Tennessee, launching my own court reporting business (which was doing remarkable, by the way), and so on. And then just like that, she named *it*.

As she began the explanation of what she believed was happening to me, I could hardly believe what I was hearing. It was like rocket science to me at first, or rather like she was speaking a foreign language. However, the more she explained it, the more it began to make complete sense.

This doctor that I was pouring my heart out to looked at me across her desk and matter-of-factly said, "You are having anxiety attacks, also known as panic attacks." There it was. Someone had finally given *it* a name!

I was certain I had heard the words *panic attack* before, but I never really understood what those words meant. I had never needed to—until now. My initial responses began to flow. How could that be? I mean, I was not a nervous person. I didn't feel stressed out. I was not a panicky person. I was definitely not depressed! In addition to those initial responses, and even more importantly, I was a strong Christian! My reasoning continued. I have a great marriage and two beautiful children and a booming business. My husband was having a blast pursuing his musician's dream. Aren't panic attacks for people with serious problems? I could not, for the life of me, wrap my brain around what I was being forced to process. Why would I be having panic attacks? It just didn't make sense.

I could see her kindly nodding her head, almost as if she had heard these kinds of responses before. Then she thoroughly began to explain to me in greater detail all about panic attacks and anxiety and why my body was experiencing what it was.

The more she spoke, the more obvious it was that she was right. It totally made sense. While I thought my life was similar to drinking from a water fountain on a warm summer day, the reality was my emotions and body were trying to take in the flood of water from a fire hydrant coming right at me.

This doctor wisely shared with me how my move from Florida, leaving everything and everyone I ever knew, then launching my own successful business, working hard at being a good wife and a loving mother, plus the traumatic circumstances that had happened with our daughter, all of these were key factors in causing my body and emotions to wreak havoc on me. In other words, it may have taken a while, but finally after all this time, this was how my body was handling all of those circumstances and challenges and emotions. Everything—the good and the bad—had been bottled up inside me and was now taking its toll on my emotions and my body in the form of full-blown panic attacks.

She compared my body to a Styrofoam cup. All the good things in my life, along with all the bad things, had caused my cup—my life—to be filled to the brim. Then when these different circum-stances came along that I had walked through (the move from Florida, the launch of my business, the trauma at the Celebration Station, and the febrile seizures that my baby girl had), they were like big holes being poked into the sides of my cup. Just like a poked Styrofoam cup would begin to leak, my emotions had reached their max, and my body was responding the only way it knew how. I was experiencing panic attacks. I may have thought my life was great on the outside, but on the inside, my emotions had been on a roll-er-coaster ride for quite a while. Finally, my body was catching up to that ride. It was saying *enough already!*

I really don't remember much more about that doctor's appointment other than her diagnosing me with having panic attacks and her offering me a prescription for antidepressant medicine. Without making a big fuss, I respectfully declined the offer of that prescription. I wanted to process this new information, and I certainly didn't feel depressed. Perhaps now that I had learned exactly what *it* was that I was dealing with, I would now have a better grasp on how to battle and overcome it. Plus, I knew sharing this insightful information with my husband would be helpful for both of us. After all, I didn't feel like a panicky person, so I assumed I could figure this out easily, now that I had a clearer understanding of what was going on.

Unfortunately, my panic attacks didn't stop. In fact, it seemed they were only getting worse. They didn't happen every day, but they did happen often enough to affect my life in so many ways.

Off to the Emergency Room

I remember the first time I had my husband take me to the ER. This time I was definitely convinced I was having a heart attack in addition to an anxiety attack. My husband lovingly obliged. I know he could tell how serious it was when I explained that this time there was something more going on. To this day, I cannot think of the appropriate words to adequately describe the speed of my heartbeats and the awkward, bizarre, and familiar (yet unfamiliar) condition I was experiencing. Of course, the enormous amount of fear that strangled me whenever this would happen was in its own category.

To my surprise, my husband's suspicions were correct. It was indeed just another one of my horribly scary panic attacks. The hospital doctor told me the tests he ran came back normal and that I was experiencing another anxiety attack. He wrote me a script for some medicine—another offer for an antidepressant. I felt frustrated and disappointed because I wanted these attacks to stop, and I didn't want to turn to medicine for them to stop.

I totally respect and understand that these medical doctors were doing what they felt best to do by offering me some medicines to keep my body and mind calm so that I would no longer experience these attacks at the rate that I was. However, with my strong-willed (or perhaps stubborn) nature, I once again declined the doctor's prescription. Something deep inside me gave me the faith and determination to keep crying out to the Lord for complete healing. I just knew He could and would heal me.

Finally, I had a new fervency to conquer these attacks, and a serious fight mentally began to rise up in me. If I was going to decline what the doctors were offering, then I realized I had better be ready for a season of serious spiritual warfare and prayer. Little did I know the depth of battle that was in front of me and the lessons I would learn along the way.

Just Another Afternoon

One afternoon, just a couple weeks later, I was at home in our adorable country home in Tennessee. If memory serves me correctly, my kids were upstairs taking a nap. I was standing in front of the sink washing dishes. Then lo and behold, without much warning, it happened again.

It has been years since that very day, but I can clearly remember what I experienced that particular day like it was yesterday. My heart began to race, and it was racing faster than I could handle. My body was shaking uncontrollably. I was feeling horribly strange all over. Nothing inside my body felt right or normal, and I definitely was not in control of what was happening to me. I felt like my life was going to end in those moments. I was sure I was going to die right there on my kitchen floor.

While I was experiencing this crazy anxiety attack right there in my kitchen, I did something unusual for me. All I could think to do in that moment of sheer panic was immediately get in a fetal position on the cold, hardwood kitchen floor. It actually took every ounce of sanity and reasonable thinking for me to muster the idea to do that. As I lay there, I began to weep uncontrollably. I mean uncontrollably! I continued to weep and weep and weep. Actually, it was more of a heaving cry of desperation that was coming out of the depths of my soul. Every part of my mind and body was gripped in absolute fear, terror, and panic. I really thought I was losing my mind.

I began to cry out to God in a way I never had before. Oh, I had cried, and I had prayed. But this time was different. It was a cry from the deepest places of absolute dependence on the One who created me. This wasn't just a cry of pity or panic. This was a cry of absolute desperation, pleading for God to deliver me from these vicious attacks.

As I continued lying there on that cold floor in my fetal position, I begged God to let me live with every ounce of faith and strength I had. I called on the name of Jesus with the honor and authority that I knew I could as His child.

Everything in me wanted to live the abundant life that Jesus had promised us in His word. After all, it is the thief, the enemy, who came to steal, kill, and destroy, not Jesus (John 10:10)! I knew my God was able to see me through this battle. In those moments on the floor, I began to not just pray but believe that He would answer my desperate cry for help.

I'm not sure how long I lay on the kitchen floor that day, but it was the first time since these attacks started that I got what I felt was a clear and literal assurance from the Lord that He was hearing my cries; He was giving me a promise that I would get through this victoriously.

As I lay there on my kitchen floor that afternoon, I saw a vision of myself (which had never happened to me before). In this vision, I clearly saw my husband on a stage behind a pulpit, and I was standing beside him. I also saw our two children on the stage with us. In my vision, our children were much older. Of course, I had no clue what that vision really meant, but I immediately felt an incredible peace come over me. I had no doubt that the Lord was showing me a promise. He wasn't finished with me! Relief swept over me. Once my body calmed down, I was finally able to regain my composure and normalcy for the rest of that day. As relieved as I felt in that moment, looking back, I realize now how exceptionally significant that vision was for me that day. I had absolutely no idea what the Lord had planned nor the journey that was yet to unfold in front of me. Obviously, the Lord did.

If I Could Touch the Hem of His Garment

M y husband had joined the worship team at the church we were attending in Knoxville, Tennessee. It was a church of about eight hundred people. On this particular morning, my husband had gone to the church earlier than me and the kids to rehearse with the worship team before service. I checked our kids into the children's ministry classes, and I randomly decided to sit on the left side of the large sanctuary, about midway back, just as the worship service began. I could see my husband up on the stage, guitar in hand, and I felt excited for the service to begin.

I have always loved the praise-and-worship portion of the church service. Any opportunity to worship the Lord in that way is a gift to me. This day was even more special because my husband had just joined the worship team and was honored to be a part of this incredible ministry.

It was the second or third song in, as I was singing alongside hundreds of other worshippers, all of a sudden, out of nowhere, a panic attack began to happen. Like a furious tornado coming without warning, the storm in my body began to spin out of control. My heart began to beat out of my chest as that bizarre feeling that I had become so familiar with began to consume me all over. I simply did not know what to do.

We were still somewhat new to this church, and I really didn't know anyone there. I hadn't had time to make any friends there yet. I realized, as this attack began to consume me, that there were strangers to my right and strangers to my left. Of course, they were church-going strangers, but no one I would feel comfortable bothering in a moment such as this.

Everyone around me was oblivious to the attack I was experiencing in those moments as the worship team continued to lead in worship. I was doing all I could to hold it together. I remember grabbing a hold of the back of the pews—or were they chairs? I don't even remember. I just remember saying to God, "Lord, please, not here at church, not in the middle of worship!" It's one thing for this to happen when I'm at home or with my husband somewhere nearby, but not in church when I'm surrounded by strangers.

I feel like a broken record when I say that every time one of these attacks happened, I became convinced I was about to die. My head would scream one thing, telling me logically to remember it's just another panic attack. All the while, the rest of my body was convincing me that this could be the moment I die and see Jesus face to face.

Even though my husband was in the same room, it felt like he was a million miles away way up on that stage. If this was happening at home with my husband around, I could ask him to hold me and pray over me while I shook and trembled and tried to steady my heart back. But that was obviously not the case.

I remember lowering my head as I began to weep as quietly as I could. In that moment, all I could think to do was get down on my knees in the midst of hundreds of people and just cry out to the Lord in my desperation. I was fearful and felt out of control with what was happening to me. The worship music was loud (for which I was grateful). I didn't want to draw any attention to myself.

As I was on my knees, crying out to the Lord, I thought about how desperate the woman in the Bible with the issue of blood must have felt trying to touch Jesus as she was surrounded by hundreds of others trying to touch Him. I thought how determined she must have been in the midst of a huge crowd of people to press through to Him. She knew she just needed to touch the hem of Jesus's garment, and she would be healed. So in that moment, that's exactly how I prayed. I whispered those very words as I was kneeling there, face down, eyes full of tears, "Jesus, if only I could just touch the hem of your garment like the woman with the issue of blood, I would be healed." That's all I could say, and apparently in that moment, that was all I needed to say.

After a few moments passed, the worship mood began to change even though my heart rate did not. The singers had paused their singing as the musicians still continued to play softly. Then something absolutely miraculous happened. It was something so wonderful, so marvelous, that I could hardly believe my ears. To this day, I am still amazed at how awesome and personal God truly is.

I was still on my knees trying to calm myself and breathe normal as a woman's voice began to speak loudly over the music. She was somewhere over on the right side of the sanctuary, several rows away from me. I could not see her, but I could definitely hear her. She began to speak loudly and gave a simple but profound prophetic word that was so clear and so direct. The worship music continued to play beautifully in the background as she said these words I will never forget: The Lord wants to say to you, "If you would just touch the hem of My garment, you will be healed!"

I couldn't believe what I was hearing. Did she really just say those exact words—the very words I just cried out to Jesus? Yes, she had! I could hardly contain myself. I could hardly believe it. But I had to believe it. Right in the middle of literally hundreds and hundreds of people, in the middle of a time of worship, the Lord had given this woman the very words that shot an immeasurable amount of hope right into my soul. My God had heard me in my desperation, and He was speaking directly and personally right to me. He was confirming, once again, that He and I would get through this together. He was going to heal me indeed!

I remember slowly standing up, as if expecting hundreds of eyes to be on me because everyone would know that that word was for me because I was the one who was desperately praying those exact words. But no one was looking. No one was paying attention to me at all. I wasn't the spectacle that I thought I was. Everyone around me had their eyes closed and hands lifted, just savoring this moment in the Lord's presence. Meanwhile, all I could do was stand in utter amazement because of what the Lord had just done. He met me right there in that crowd as I pressed through. Perhaps, no one else in that room had a clue what just happened, but my God heard me! And He answered me!

To say that I stood and worshiped with reckless abandon would be an understatement. I couldn't wait for my husband to get off that stage so I could share this miraculous moment with him. I had to fight the urge to run up there on that stage and share what God had just done for me with everyone in the congregation. However, I knew this was a special moment between me and the Lord. He knew those were the very words I needed to hear and the very promise I needed to cling to.

As the torrential storms of these attacks continued on and on throughout the next few months, that's exactly what I did. I clung to those words.

The Move Back Home

After a few years of living in Tennessee, my husband and I had been praying about the direction the Lord wanted us to take in our lives. My court reporting business was going extremely well while doors were opening up for my husband's music career. Our son was finishing up kindergarten, and we were enjoying the ministry we were a part of. We had begun a Bible study in our home for our neighbors, and it was going great. Even though I was struggling personally with these anxiety attacks, the Lord was at work, and miracles were happening in our neighbors' lives. For some reason, however, we felt a new season was just around the corner for us.

The phone call came unexpectedly. The new pastor of the church we attended back in Florida was calling. He had recently been set in as the lead pastor there at our home church and shared that he and his wife had heard many things about us. He asked if we would fly down to meet with them, possibly to consider moving back to Florida and coming on staff at the church we so loved.

It was an instant yes for both of us since we had been sensing that God was leading us in a different direction already. Those few years in Tennessee were definitely maturing years for us, but when this phone call came, we knew the Lord was leading us right back to where we belonged.

I was also quite sure it was right where I would find healing and finally be whole again. I was convinced I had been a fish out of water for this last season, and I was ready to be where I belonged again.

We moved back home with the grandest of homecomings from family and friends and jumped right back into full-time ministry.

The new pastors there easily became the dearest of friends. Life felt so good again. It felt so right. No doubt, I loved being back home! However, my battle was, unfortunately, still in full swing.

My panic attacks kept coming. For some crazy and unexplainable reason, they even got stronger, becoming more frequent and feeling way more intense. I began to feel as if I was under a big, dark cloud that would not go away. I couldn't understand. I was finally back home among family and friends, doing life with amazing people all around me, which was so comforting. So why were these panic attacks intensifying?

I began to feel like I was going crazy. I felt like I was losing my mind. What was wrong with me? At random times, day and night, my anxiety would become so great within me. The storm I was in kept brewing stronger and stronger. I simply could not wrap my mind around it. My marriage was good, my kids were healthy, and I was back HOME for goodness sake! Why was this happening? Why wouldn't this stop? Not only was this debilitating to me, it was also embarrassing. I felt like no one would or could understand me.

I became concerned that my husband was questioning what he had signed up for when he married me. I began to feel insecure, assuming he was thinking his wife was losing her marbles. (Of course, I was thinking the same thing about myself.) There were hours—sometimes entire days—when I was entirely debilitated. I couldn't even function. I felt overwhelmed in so many ways because I knew I was healthy from all outward appearances. The doctors had even confirmed it.

From the outside looking in, life seemed good. All the while, I was silently suffering on the inside, being gripped by crippling fear, convinced that I could die at any moment when one of these attacks would come. It was as if more days than not, I was paralyzed by fear and anxiety. I was sick and tired of feeling this way! However, I was still determined not to take medicine of any kind because I wanted to do this with Jesus. There were too many stories from the Bible of Jesus healing people, including the woman with the issue of blood, which was my promise too. I also knew of many personal testimonies of people being miraculously healed. So I continued to hold on and believe for my own healing.

I knew the promises in His word were true. I wanted to persevere no matter what things felt or looked like in the natural. I had become convinced, whether I lived or died, I still would win in the end. Of course, I really did want to live!

My husband remained patient and gracious during these crazy episodes. All we knew to do was cry out to Jesus, which is exactly what we did…every…single…time. In the middle of the night when another attack would come, all I had to do was tap my husband's arm and say, "It's happening" or "Hold me," and he knew exactly what that meant. He would wrap his arms around me and begin to pray out loud over me. As my heart would race uncontrollably, my teeth would be clattering loudly, and my entire body would be shaking from head to toe. And David would continue to pray over me until the attack would leave. These attacks filled me with paralyzing fear and frustration, but they would eventually dissipate, and relief would come.

It was tiring, to say the least. But with my husband believing with me, we were not going to give up or give in.

One night I had just made dinner and set everything out on the table. I called my kids and husband to the table. We had said our prayer together over dinner, and I had just eaten my first bite. Then it started. When the anxiety attack began, I reached for my husband's hand and squeezed it. He gave me that knowing look, and I excused myself from the table to go lie down on the couch.

It wasn't long before my kids were finished with dinner and coming over to the couch asking why I didn't eat my dinner with them. For some reason, this attack seemed worse than any of the other ones I had. I suddenly began to weep as my children were talking to me, and I began to tell them that Mommy wasn't feeling good. I shared with them that if something happened to Mommy, I wanted them to remember that I loved them and that I wanted them to always live for Jesus. My husband heard me and came over looking at me intently. I felt like this might be the end. My heart was racing so fast, I didn't know if I could live through it. My body was out of control and fear had gripped me so tightly, I felt like its weakest victim on the planet.

There was still no logical reason this kept happening to me. I was beyond ready to be free. As desperate as I was to live life to the fullest, in those moments, I wasn't sure that I would. After a little while that evening, my husband carried me to our bedroom and laid me down. I could not stop shaking. My heart continued to race, and as the hours kept circling the clock that night, a new level of anxiety hovered above my head.

A Fight for My Life

It had to be about 2:00 or 3:00 a.m. I had been attempting to sleep for many hours, but sleep wouldn't come that night. I was doing my best to convince myself that this, too, would eventually pass. It had to. It took a long time, but I had finally calmed down just enough to doze off for a bit when suddenly I woke right up again in the middle of another full-blown panic attack. Once again, as my routine had been, I began to pray and cry out to Jesus as I shook uncontrollably, and my heart beat wildly inside of my chest.

This night was indeed different. This night was even more intense. This time I could hardly catch my breath. I was really having difficulty breathing. In that moment, I could tangibly feel something—a demon, no doubt—wrapping its hands around my neck as if to try to choke me. Fear had me in its grip in the most controlling way. I was in a fight for my life, and I felt I was losing it!

Just when I didn't think it could get worse, a fiercer level of panic set in. I woke my husband up, and we fervently cried out to Jesus together. No doubt, I was in the greatest spiritual warfare battle of my life. After a few moments of our loud, fervent, and intense prayers *in the name of Jesus*, that demonic attack stopped, and I was suddenly and miraculously feeling an incredible peace.

Trusting God

As the weeks continued, I was learning to trust in God's word and the power of the name of Jesus. I was trusting Him for my very life and breath in a way I never had before. I was definitely learning to persevere through the toughest season of my adult life thus far.

As horribly difficult as all this was, I was at least grateful to have an idea of what it was that I was dealing with. When I was feeling good, I was feeling good. I would continue to go about my days living life in as much normalcy as possible under the circumstances. I kept reminding myself that the promises in the Bible were true for me. I knew that there was power in prayer and that God was hearing me. I believed that God's ears were attentive to the prayers of the righteous (Psalm 34:15, 1 Peter 3:12 NIV). And because of my relationship with Jesus Christ, I had been made the righteousness of God (2 Corinthians 5:21 NIV). No doubt, His ears were attentive to my cries for mercy.

I was maturing in my personal relationship with the Lord. I knew my life was in His hands. Psalm 139:16 (NIV) had become my favorite verse: All the days ordained for me were written in Your book before one of them came to be. I began to realize that He was the one in control, not me. He was my strong tower that I could run to and find shelter. He was becoming my soul's greatest satisfaction, my true source of life and hope and healing. I clung to the words of Jesus: But if you remain in me, and my words remain in you, you may ask for anything you want, and it will be granted (John 15:7 NLT)! I was not about to let go of that promise.

It was easy for me to feel strong and courageous when I was not having a panic attack. The real test—along with my weakness—showed up when I was having one. I would remind myself every time that it would be over soon. I reflected on how far he had brought me, how faithful the Lord was every time I called out to Him through one of these attacks. All the while I continued to ask the Lord to reveal to me why this was happening. Desperately, I wanted to do whatever I needed to do to get victory from these attacks once and for all.

Another time an attack came in the middle of the night, and I pleaded for my husband to take me to the hospital. I physically and emotionally could not stand what I was feeling inside my body anymore. My heart was beating so fast—this time, even my husband was afraid for my life. My mother came over right away to watch our kids, and he took me to the emergency room.

After running several different tests, I was told once again what we already knew. (You think I would have been convinced by now that there would be no other answer.) The hospital just confirmed what we already knew. I was experiencing another anxiety attack. Then as the story goes, I was offered another antidepressant prescription. And once again, I declined. I simply did not want to turn to medicine. I would continue to turn to Jesus.

According to the Bible, if the Son sets you free, you will be free indeed (John 8:36 NIV). That freedom was for me just as it was for all others who truly trust in the name of Jesus. I was going to take God at His word. To some, this may seem extremely foolish but not to me. I had to do what I felt the Lord wanted me to do. This was my journey. I had to trust Him even through the darkest of seasons. He was going to see me through this storm, I was sure of it. Because of that assurance, I stayed determined to continue to stand and fight every step of the way.

As difficult and as scary as it was, I was convinced that God had a lesson and a plan for me through all of this. It wasn't easy one bit. There were plenty of days I wanted to throw in the towel. In the depths of my soul, however, I had faith enough to believe that I would get through this horrific storm, and I would indeed be an overcomer.

For my own faith to grow (not to mention my sanity), I had to continue to trust that God was at work in my life. I prayed and worshipped my way through day by day. Even in the darkest moments, I chose to remain steadfast and cry out to Jesus with every fiber of my being. I knew that one day, one way or another, I was going to see freedom from these attacks because God would lead me to victory. I was sure of it.

The weeks went by, and the attacks continued to come when I least expected them. I would go days feeling *normal* and get back into a regular routine with my family and with work. Then it would come again. One early evening, as I was cooking dinner, boiling water on the stove, another panic attack came. I had to call a nearby friend to come over and help me finish cooking the meal because my body was doing its thing, and I could not even function. I literally couldn't even stir my rice! A few days later, I had to ask that same friend to pick up my children from school because my husband was in a meeting, and my nervous system was a wreck. There was no way I would even be able to drive that day.

The holidays rolled around, and our church worship team would be performing a special Christmas show on the big stage at the mall. I was so excited to go with my family and friends to enjoy this occasion especially because my husband was one of the lead singers.

My kids and I arrived at the mall, and we headed over to the side of the mall where the performance would be taking place. Then suddenly without warning, right there in the middle of the mall, it happened. I had to quickly ask a friend to stand by my kids so I could sit calmly and fight my way through the panic without making a scene for myself. I just wanted this horrible attack to pass. The defeat, humiliation, frustration, disappointment, and fear that always accompanied these attacks were all in tow, screaming loudly as I hung my head and prayed fervently for them to go. I kept hearing my husband's words: This one will pass too. You will live, Dina. Just let it pass. In Jesus's name! As I cried out to Jesus, those words once again proved true.

The Final Straw

It was the last day of school before Christmas break. Both of our children were performing in their Christmas play at their elementary school. The kids had been working on this play for many weeks, and my son had a major role in the play. Our dearest friends (our pastor and his wife, David and Cheree Wright, who we were on staff with) were with us watching their daughter perform as well.

The video cameras were ready to capture our adorable kids in their big show. The first well-rehearsed Christmas song was sung, and all the kids looked adorable all dressed up in their special Christmas outfits. Another song had just ended, and everyone in the audience began to clap with smiles beaming across their faces. In that moment, my intention was to be doing the same thing as every other proud parent in that auditorium. However, as I began to lift my arms up to erupt in applause, my body suddenly went numb from the neck down. Totally numb. My heart began to beat horrifically fast, and the all-too-familiar weird, bizarre feeling I had come too acquainted with now hit me again.

I was devastated. Here I was, sitting in the middle of my kids' Christmas play, and I couldn't even clap my hands to applaud them. My hands lay limp in my lap, and my head lay on my husband's shoulder. I couldn't believe this was happening—or could I?—right here, right now. To make matters worse, the attack lasted for the entirety of the show. When the show was over, I couldn't even walk on my own two feet out to our car. It was as if my entire nervous and muscular system had shut down. I couldn't function. My husband

and our pastor, one on each side, had to hold me up and carry me all the way out to the car. When I got to the car, all I could do was weep.

This was the final straw. This time I had had it!

I was an emotional and physical wreck all the way back to their house. When we arrived at our pastor's house, there were two other couples who had been called to come and pray over me. Apparently, they all had *had it* too! Everyone was in agreement that enough was enough. I felt like I was at the end of my rope, and those who loved me felt the same way. They were ready to go into battle with me and pray me through. And for the next few hours, that's exactly what they did!

The prayer of a righteous person is powerful and effective (James 5:16 NIV). That was the verse they were standing on, believing that their prayers for me would be powerful and effective. I was truly grateful to have this army of prayer warriors around me on this night.

As I lay there weeping, weak and frail, I was so grateful for the fervent prayers that were being raised to heaven on my behalf. I don't remember a lot of specifics about that night, but I do remember a lot of intense praying and intercession happening on my behalf. As exhausting as the night was, it definitely filled me with hope that the Lord would bring my healing.

Worship, My Weapon

For the duration of another entire year, these attacks continued. Whether I was in the grocery store, out to dinner with friends, enjoying some couch time with my husband, working at the church office, it simply did not matter. The panic attacks still came. As difficult as they were when they were happening, I had become even more determined to cling stronger and harder to the One who I knew could and would heal me. I just had to continue to stand, as Paul reminds us, for it is by your own faith that you stand firm (2 Corinthians 1:24 NLT).

I now understand why the Bible tells us to put on the full armor of God so that when the day of evil comes, you may be able to stand your ground, and after you have done everything, to stand (Ephesians 6:13 NIV). So stand is what I did. I knew there was power released every time I declared the name of Jesus over my life. So I continued to pray as if my life depended on it. Because it did. I was still in the greatest battle of my life.

Worship became my weapon of choice. If there was a way to attach worship music to me like an IV drip, I would have done it. Day or night, when my body was struggling, when my breathing was difficult, or when fear would grip me, I would turn on worship songs that would fill my mind, my heart, and my soul with praises and promises about the God I knew was able to heal me. I had to constantly put God above my circumstances. Singing songs of worship allowed me do just that.

There were some days when all I was able to do was lie on the floor in a fetal position. On those days, it was guaranteed that worship music was on, and it was washing over me like a much-needed rain in a desert place. Day after day, I became more and more aware that the Lord was indeed carrying me every step of the way through this journey. He was also ever-so-gently revealing things about me to me that I now realize would not have happened any other way.

There were a few songs that became like medicine to my weary soul. The one that truly became my anthem (and the inspiration for this book title) was by the late Rich Mullins. The song was "Hold Me Jesus," and the chorus to this song became a lifeline for me. It was as if the song had been written just for me. To this very day, those words I sang so desperately way back then still bring me great comfort today.

> So hold me, Jesus, 'cause I'm shaking like a leaf.
> You have been King of my glory;
> won't you be my prince of peace.

While I was still believing that victory would come for me, I had also become very battle-weary. I felt as if I was living a nightmare that was stuck on repeat. My mind and my body were telling me different things. My spirit was willing to fight, but my flesh was weak. I had to keep a song in my heart and on my lips, day after day and night after night. As the Psalmist said: My heart, O God, is steadfast; I will sing and make music with all my soul (Psalm 108:1 NIV) and My flesh and my heart may fail, but God is the strength of my heart and my portion forever (Psalm 73:26 NIV). I was doing all I knew to do to cling to those words.

One Saturday afternoon when my body was struggling to find its normal and I was once again feeling overwhelmed by the effects of an anxiety attack, I asked my husband to take me to my parents' house. I needed a change of scenery. My mom was gracious enough to set me up on their water bed. She dimmed the lights real low, laid out the fluffiest pillows, and put a Hillsong Worship CD on repeat. I lay there for hours that day, worshipping the Lord, crying out to the Lord, determined to win this battle through Him and Him alone. I don't know who I was convincing more, me or Him, but I stayed fervent in my prayers for the Lord to heal me and set me free.

The Change—From the Inside Out

I found myself more and more often needing to lie down in a fetal position listening to worship songs over and over. Finally, something started changing for me. The change wasn't immediate, but something was taking place inside of me that I couldn't explain if I tried. God was doing something on the inside of me that was beyond what I could yet understand.

As the months went by, and these life-altering attacks came and went, something was truly taking place in the depths of my very own soul. I was discovering a side to the God I thought I knew. I was learning to understand and see the father's heart of God. I gained a deeper resolve of trust for Him alone. It was as if I was being born again…again. I had given my life to Jesus as a fifteen-year-old teenager after seeing my mom surrender her life to the Lord the year before. But this season, for me, was much different. This was deeper. This was tangible. This was personally intimate.

My relationship with the Lord had been genuine. I had been serving the Lord faithfully since giving my life to Jesus at the age of fifteen. Yet I felt like I was finally learning the truth about God's character and my responsibility to stand on His promises. As horrific as these storms were, I was growing and maturing in a way I had never thought necessary up until this season of my life. Something finally began to click. My eyes and ears were opening up in a greater way.

I was learning how to let go of things that I didn't have answers to. I didn't realize until now that I was more of a control freak than I thought. I was learning how to let go of control. I was discovering how to truly hear from Him and how to experience God's peace, which exceeds anything we can understand (Philippians 4:7 NLT). I was discovering so much about the God of the Bible, who is the same yesterday, today, and forever. The depth of my personal relationship with my God became the real anchor for my soul. As painful, embarrassing, scary, and humbling as this was, I was beginning to appreciate my personal relationship with the Lord like never before.

Every single time an anxiety attack would begin, and I felt like I was about to die, I would remember that Jesus told us to speak to the mountain. He didn't tell us to look at the mountain. He didn't tell us to think about the mountain or cry about the mountain. He certainly didn't say I would be defeated by the mountain. He said to speak to it (Mark 11:23 NIV), and so speak I did.

I was personally getting to experience His strength in me when I was at my weakest. It was Him who could sustain me—my God, my Jesus—the One who filled me with His Holy Spirit so that I could have the power and strength to live my life to the fullest and overcome to the end!

Finally, I began to have a renewed spiritual fervency beyond my years of knowing Christ. I began to absorb His word in a whole new way. A new fight and tenacity began to well up in me that had never been there before. I was learning how to truly stand and persevere as we are instructed to do in Scripture. I was learning how to not only fight but win the spiritual battle that was waging war for my soul. So much was becoming clearer and clearer.

The Lord was revealing to me that in those times while I was shaking like a leaf, He really was my Prince of Peace. The Bible is not a fairy-tale history book. It is the Word of God. The Bible is filled with promises, and those promises are for those who trust Him. And I am ever so grateful I am one of those who have learned to trust Him.

Getting Unstuffed

Along with the craziness of things that I had experienced in those few previous years, I began to realize there were things from my childhood that I had stuffed down deep inside. The Lord was gracious to me as He began to heal me. No doubt, the key was that I was finally allowing Him to heal me from the inside out. I was really giving Him the full reigns of my life once and for all. All the while, He was faithfully showing me that He was the calm in the middle of my storm.

This was still, by no means, an easy battle. Every step of the way, every single attack, every single episode of those debilitating and tormenting things was more than what I could handle in my own strength. I had to dig down deep and take hold of every single promise that was for God's children. I did not want to just know about God, I wanted to know Him. And I wanted to keep praying those fervent prayers that were effective and availed much.

I was realizing that as God's child, I had every right to approach His throne of grace with boldness. So with greater boldness and faith, I came. My prayers for freedom and victory were happening boldly and loudly day after day as I was taking Him at His word.

I kept singing worship music all day, every day, and all night every night. I would wake up in the night with a worship song to the Lord in my mouth. Even in my weakness, I could see the overflow of my life bringing the Lord honor and praise, no matter what things felt like in the natural. Jesus had become my song, and I just had to sing!

The Depths of What I Felt

Over the years, I have tried to adequately put into words the depth of fear that would grip me in the midst of all my anxiety attacks as well as the desperation that kept me fighting. Although I have written on these pages about much of my journey, I still feel I have only touched the surface of what my body, mind, and emotions were entangled in. However, more than describing the depths of despair in more detail, I'd rather adequately share how worshipping God passionately in the midst of great darkness is an absolute lifeline for survival and victory—that you can be sure of.

Knowing there is a God in heaven who keeps my prayers like incense before His throne (Revelation 8:4 NLT), what more comfort would I need? It's definitely promises like that that kept me holding on and kept me afloat. Declaring God's praises through worship, praying, reading His word, and then believing those promises were for me where the power to overcome came from.

Through it all, in the deepest anguish of my soul, there was always still a small voice giving me enough peace to keep me going. All I knew to do was continue to pray my way through, sing my way through, worship my way through, sing a little louder, worship a little longer, pray without ceasing! And that's exactly what I did. Then, as I did week after week, month after month, my strength in the Lord grew stronger and stronger. In the waking hours of the day and in the wee hours of the night, Jesus became my passion and my song.

God's word became my medicine. What powerful life-changing medicine it was—the purest medicine there is. Scriptures like Psalm 94:19 (NIV)—When anxiety was great within me, your consolation brought joy to my soul—were what kept my faith growing and still do to this day.

In addition to my pursuit of victory through worship, prayer, and God's Word, I, myself, was humble enough to realize my need for others to know that I was not all right. My closest companions were helping to carry me along when my arms were too heavy to lift up. I had to allow others to pray for me through this journey to the finish line.

The Real Super Bowl Champ

It was Super Bowl Sunday, and the year was 2000. I was never a fanatical football fan growing up, but when you marry a man who played Pee Wee football all the way up to college, you learn to enjoy the game.

I don't remember who was at our house that evening, and I don't remember which teams were playing. I do remember sitting on the floor with my back leaned up against the couch behind me. The Super Bowl was on, and the game was intense. I couldn't tell you which quarter during the game *it* happened, but *it* happened again while I was surrounded by family and friends. So once again, I cried out to Jesus.

Somehow in that moment, I knew this anxiety attack was different. It was different because that Super Bowl Sunday was an end to over a three-year battle that I had been in. It was the day victory came for me. On that Super Bowl Sunday, I had my last full-blown panic attack. The Los Angeles Rams brought home the Super Bowl trophy that year, but I felt like I was the real victor that night. I was the winner gleaming in victory on that night, and Jesus was my MVP.

Honestly, I didn't know quite yet that breakthrough had truly come for me that night. It was only when day after day, night after night, week after week, I began to feel free—truly free. There was a new peace in my soul, and I began to feel truly whole. I was finally released from the snare that had entangled me during those previous few years. I was finally experiencing the miraculous fruit of all those laboring prayers from me and those who fought alongside me and loved me well in the fiercest storm of my life.

I took each *normal* day as a great gift. I had learned so much about myself and so much about the Lord. I really began to feel like a brand-new person. There were things that God had taught me in that season that I never even realized I needed to learn. There were secret places in my heart that needed healing that only God knew about. He had indeed healed me—body, soul, mind, and spirit.

He Makes All Things New

L ittle did I know what God had in store several months down the road. It was in the fall of that same year that my husband was offered the senior pastor position at our church, Christian Life Fellowship. Only then, in hindsight, did I begin to appreciate, in a deeper way, what the Lord had brought me through. It was as if the Holy Spirit confirmed to me that although it was painful beyond words what I had walked through, the Lord allowed this necessary season to prepare me for the years of full-time pastoral ministry that lay ahead for us.

The lessons I learned, the faith I gained, the reliance on God's Word, the joy of His presence, and the power of prayer that I experienced firsthand had become priceless to me. Worshipping Him through song had truly become a weapon and a treasure that I couldn't live without! There was always a song in my heart and on my lips. Just as there still is today!

Morning, noon, or night, you will hear worship music playing around me. Whether I'm walking my dog, going for a run, taking a shower, driving in my car, putting on my makeup, cooking dinner—you name it—worship music is playing. No matter where I am or what I'm doing, I live day by day reminded that it is in Him we live and move and have our being (Acts 17:28 NIV).

We Are No Different

D o not misunderstand. I was already a worshipper of God before these panic attacks came. I loved to be in God's presence, worshipping him alongside others who love him. However, the intimacy that now floods my soul in God's presence, and the privilege I feel worshipping Him now that I know Him more intimately fills me with the greatest peace and satisfaction.

As I've shared my story with friends, ministry events, and at women's conferences over the years, I am always blown away by the responses from so many people who have suffered or are still suffering from these brutal attacks. From someone who at one time didn't even know what a panic attack or anxiety attack was, it's easy for me to quickly become like family with others who are all too familiar with them. I understand the comfort of speaking to someone who has walked this journey of great torment, and who has had to fight for their life.

We are no different. Each and every one of us has been given life by a God who loves us greatly. So much so that He sent His son, Jesus Christ, into the world to prove it. Not only did Jesus prove God's love for us, He also paid a great price for our freedom. The Bible tells us that God does not show favoritism (Romans 2:11 NLT). So since His word is filled with life-giving promises for those who love and obey Him, then we should all live to make way for those promises to be a reality in each of our lives.

More Than Coping

The most commonly asked questions I get are, *Why didn't you just take the medicine to help you cope along the way?* and *Is it true you never took any medicine to help control these attacks or balance out your emotions?* The fact of the matter is, I never did take one pill or prescription to deal with the anxiety I was suffering from. I certainly could have, and a few times it was a serious consideration. However, I had determined in my heart that I simply did not want to take any medicine. I wanted God to heal me. It was as simple as that. I certainly do not judge those who have chosen to use medicine. This was simply and profoundly my journey. As dark and difficult as those days were, looking back now, I still would not have changed a thing. The faith I gained and the confidence in God's love and mercy I came to understand were well worth the price I had to pay to get through. I know I sowed in tears, but I have also reaped with joy (Psalm 126:5 NIV).

The reason I wrote this book was to share this testimony of God's great work in my life. This is part of my story. I have no doubt it was a storm that I had to walk through with the Lord. It was brutal, debilitating, frightening, and somewhat embarrassing for sure. What the enemy meant for destruction, though, God definitely turned around for my good. This journey has made me the woman I am today—a woman who knows where her strength comes from. Undoubtedly, I can say my strength comes from the Lord.

It became quite obvious to me, as the months and years unfolded, that the lessons about perseverance and fervency are ones that will help sustain me for the rest of my life. I had to learn the hard way, as many do, how to let go and let God. My life really is in His hands.

I certainly don't think it was by chance or coincidence that it was exactly nine months after my last panic attack—the amount of time it takes for a new birth to take place—that my husband was set in place as the lead pastor of Christian Life Fellowship, the very place we still joyfully serve, side by side, all these years later. The role and responsibilities that we carry, as lead pastors, would have sunk me if I had not learned what I did back then about the mighty God I serve. Believing in God is one thing. Living surrendered to Him and living like your life depends on Him (because it does) is something very different.

Second Corinthians 10:4 (NKJV) says: For the weapons of our warfare are not carnal but mighty in God for pulling down strongholds. Notice it says those weapons are mighty *in* God. That is an important key to understand how to attain victory, whatever the battle may be. I have become well acquainted in the most personal way that I can only do something *mighty* when my life is in His mighty strong hands!

I would be lying if I said I've never had another moment of anxiety well up within me over these passed many years since that Super Bowl Sunday. That is simply not true. However, I can honestly say that I have not had to deal with any full-blown panic or anxiety attacks as I did during those three long years.

While I have still walked through very difficult trials throughout the years, I am grateful to say that anxiety no longer takes its toll on me as it did those years ago. Since learning how to fight the good fight (1 Timothy 1:18 ISV) through worship, prayer, and standing on God's promises, I've been able to trust God in all circumstances while clinging to my faith. I remain grateful for His faithfulness each and every time. Certainly, I still have my share of days when it is a struggle to catch my breath, when my anxious thoughts get the best of me, and when my emotions feel wrecked. That's when I remember that the Spirit of Him who raised Jesus from the dead is living in me (Romans 8:11 NIV).

The Story Goes On

M y husband and I were busy raising our family and leading our church. We had outgrown our church building (with some Sundays standing room only), and we were finally able to take a leap of faith to build a brand-new church facility in a wonderful location in our city. God was moving mightily, and our church was growing rapidly. Of course, just like in any ministry, there were many challenges and storms that came blowing through in that season. Building a new church facility on fifteen acres of land is no joke. On top of that, soon after we began building, the economy crashed right after we broke ground on our building project. At one point on the news, our very city was named the number one city in all of America with home foreclosures. So many people in our church were losing their homes, Some were losing their jobs. Many had to move out of the area. It was a stressful time to say the least. Anxieties were high all around. However, God continued to show Himself to be faithful every single step of the way. As we fasted and prayed and worshipped our way through, God was faithful to carry our family and our church through. He has never let us down. Nor would we ever expect Him to.

Had I not gone through those years of intense spiritual warfare, fighting for my very life, I would not have had the perseverance, wisdom, or strength to take that journey. I also would not have been able to walk alongside so many others dealing with life's horrific storms, including my husband who was under his own dark cloud in that season of the building project.

Perseverance is like a jacket for me. I have learned to put it on every day (just like the armor of God described in Ephesians 6:11). Whether personally or in ministry, whatever challenges come, I choose to worship the Lord and pray my way through.

There have been many nights over the years where I found myself in my closet crying out to God in the wee hours of the night. Those were times of great trial, times when I was greatly burdened for the people that I love by the things that could only be resolved by the power of God alone. What a gift it is to know that I serve a God who does not slumber (Psalm 121:3 NLT). No matter the time of day, my God is listening, and because I know that to be so intimately true, I have done my best to not allow anxiety to well up within me anymore. I simply take it to the One who I know can handle it.

Chloe Bree

The year was now 2011. My younger sister, Julie, had moved to Mississippi with her family. They had been there for a few years. Their youngest daughter at the time, Chloe Bree, suddenly became very ill. When my sister, who is a nurse, took her to the doctor, she was told it was just a bug of some sort. After weeks of dealing with Chloe violently vomiting, having headaches, and not feeling well, my sister was persistent to get answers.

I can still remember the afternoon that I got the phone call. It was my mother on the other line telling me that they just discovered that my little five-year-old niece had a brain tumor. My other sister, Kristal, and I made the decision to drive to Mississippi because Chloe was immediately being transferred to a children's hospital in Tennessee and would be undergoing a major brain tumor removal surgery.

The surgery was a craniotomy to remove the tumor that was crushing her cerebellum. The surgery was to be done urgently because the increase intracranial pressure was compressing her brain stem, which was life-threatening.

To say that anxieties were high in our family that day would be a huge understatement. Both my parents and my sister's in-laws were there at the hospital as well. The surgery began, and we were told it would be a fourteen-hour surgery. Talk about an emotionally exhausting day!

I was doing my best to be full of faith and at peace, hoping the rest of my family would do the same. My sister's emotional state was beyond words as she stayed glued to the hospital room phone because a nurse was calling every hour on the hour to get an update from the surgeon. All of our emotions were on a roller coaster ride. Chloe's tumor was in a very dangerous place, and the surgery was risky, to say the least, but necessary.

During the early afternoon, I returned to the hospital room after making a phone call. All of the family was sitting there nervously. I could tell tensions were extremely high. I could tell, by the conversations and the tangibly tense atmosphere, that no one could really concentrate or feel at ease because of the severity of the situation that little Chloe was experiencing. This tumor came out of nowhere. No one understood how or why, and everyone was on pins and needles, especially my sister.

I saw my sister trying to hold on to her sanity the best she could under the circumstances. I could no longer just sit there and pray silently. The nurse had just called with the latest update on Chloe Bree. She had been losing a lot of blood during the surgery. Once again, the emotions in that room were raw, and everyone was panicking. Both sets of grandparents were not doing well. Really, no one was. In a moment of desperation, I knew I had to get my sister out of that room. I gently grabbed her by the arm and told everyone else to please stay put. I didn't want anyone else from the family to follow us.

The nurse outside the door pointed us to the chapel when I asked. To this day, I find it funny that the sign on the hallway leading to the chapel stated in big letters, *Now entering the quiet zone.* Little did they know what was about to happen in that quiet little chapel! I had carried a boom box with a worship CD in hand. My intent was certainly not to be quiet in that chapel. I was ready to go to war in prayer on behalf of that child.

Fortunately for my sister and I, when we got to the chapel, no one else was in the room. I plugged in my boom box, and I began to play a worship song called "God, I Look to You" by Bethel Worship. I sat my sister down in the room and told her to just scream or cry or get on the floor, pound her fists, or do whatever it was she needed to do. I told her that I was going to play this worship song on repeat and pray fervently over Chloe and her for this next hour until the next phone call would come. So that's exactly what I did.

With great fervency, I circled that room and prayed and worshiped and prayed and worshiped and prayed. I cried out to God, asking Him to miraculously heal Chloe Bree and to see her through every moment of this surgery. I told the Lord that we were standing on His promises, declaring that she would come out and be healed in the name of Jesus. I prayed for God to guide the hands of the surgeons in that room. I prayed for God to totally restore this little girl back to life.

At some point, while I was crying out to God in fervent prayer with my sister on the floor where she was, an ever-so-sweet Catholic priest walked into the chapel. He must have heard me praying loudly. I was certain I was being too loud for the *quiet zone*. I immediately went over to him and apologized to him if we were making too much noise. I explained that my five-year-old niece was in surgery, having a brain tumor removed, and that I was compelled to bring my sister in here to pray fervently over this situation. I apologized if it was inappropriate to bring the boom box in but was hopeful he would graciously understand that I wanted to play a worship song to help calm my sister while we prayed because she had been beside herself.

To my delight, he nodded and sweetly walked over to my sister and said to her, "I think you are being covered very well in prayer by your sister. I will just leave you both alone. Stay as long as you need to." Then he smiled at me, patted me on the back, and quietly left the room. I have a feeling he had been watching and listening longer than I thought.

God certainly showed himself faithful that day by answering our prayers. Not only was Chloe Bree's brain tumor successfully removed, but every concern they had about possible paralysis and lack of brain function did not come to pass. Chloe has lived tumor-free ever since her surgery and is thriving still as I write this book all these years later. The Lord's ear was certainly attentive to our prayers that day. He carried us through that storm as we boldly approached His throne of grace. We did just what the writer of Hebrews instructs us to do: Let us then approach God's throne of grace with confidence, so that we may receive mercy and find grace to help us in our time of need (Hebrews 4:16 NIV). Another version uses the word *boldly* in how we should approach God's throne. I have no doubt I fulfilled that one for sure that day!

Right Relationship

Having peace in your life is a real treasure. I daily find myself in total dependence on the Lord for my peace of mind because I know I have a genuine relationship with the Lord. I have learned very well that the storms of life continue to come. The fiery darts of the enemy, the devil, continue to be flung my way. Even so, I also know, without a doubt, where my strength comes from. I have learned (the hard way—but I learned) how to run to the One who is my strong tower and how to stay victorious.

I cannot say this enough: There is power in the name of Jesus Christ. When Jesus said, "If you remain in me and my words remain in you, you may ask for anything you want, and it will be granted (John 15:5 NLT)," I have no doubt He meant it!

The Bible tells us that God is not a respecter of persons (Acts 10:34), which means if He can answer prayers for me, He can answer prayers for anyone who believes. His promises are for those who believe that He is who He says He is. They are for those who are in right standing with Him. In other words, you have to be in a real relationship with Him to receive the benefits of His promises.

The only way to be in a right relationship with God is to know that Jesus Christ is the Lord of your life. When Jesus is the Lord of your life, when you are in a right relationship with God the Father, the Holy Spirit lives in you, and all of God's promises are yours if you are living according to His word. Remember it was Jesus who said, "I am the vine; you are the branches. If you remain in me and I in you, you will bear much fruit. Apart from me, you can do nothing. If you do not remain in me, you are like a branch that is thrown away and withers; such branches are picked up, thrown into the fire, and burned. If you remain in me, and my words remain in you, ask whatever you wish, and it will be done for you" (John 15:5–7 NIV). Our responsibility is to remain in Jesus Christ and allow his words to remain in us, then we can ask anything according to his will, and it will be done. That's how you can have a faith that moves mountains.

One of the most important things I have learned over these last many years is that God is real, and He stays true to His word. When the Bible says that all things work together for good to those who love God, to those who are the called according to His purpose (Romans 8:28 NKJ), that's exactly what it means. Although circumstances have happened in my life that I would not have ever wanted or welcomed, I can now see how God can redeem anything. No matter what we walk through, good or bad, He can work it for the good so that we can fulfill His purpose. That's what He does for those who are in a right relationship with Him.

Take Him at His Word

God allows the knowledge of His word and the knowledge of His character to strengthen us no matter what life brings us. This is why it is imperative to meditate on His word day and night (Psalm 1:2 NLT) like the Psalmist says. I am a living proof that living according to His word is the only way to find freedom from fear and anxiety or anything else that hinders you from running the race He has for you. When I thought I was defeated and down for the count, I clung to God's word. I sang songs of praise and songs of worship that would remind me to trust the One who is able to do exceedingly, abundantly above all that we ask or think, according to the power that works in us (Ephesians 3:20 NKJ).

What a delight it is that believers in Jesus can pray and worship our way through every storm and circumstance of life. When anxiety is great with us, when we are shaking like a leaf, there is only One who can hold us together and bring us peace that is beyond anything else this world has to offer. His name is Jesus, and He is my Prince of Peace.

Conclusion

Ironically while finishing this book, a literal storm was brewing and stirring up great fear in my home state. Hurricane Irma, a category 5 hurricane, was headed right for Florida. We have had our fair share of hurricane scares over the decades, but this one was different. All the news anchors and meteorologists were calling this the largest and fiercest storm ever on record from the Atlantic Basin. Sure enough, it was headed right our way, and it was going to cover the entire state of Florida. On top of that, the threat of a horrific storm surge—one that was unheard of for our area—was also being predicted. The weather reports were not in our favor.

As Hurricane Irma was heading for us, I had to take everything I have written about in this book and put it into practice. I was facing another storm—and this time, it was a very literal one!

Now, my husband is quite a hero in my opinion—a superman of sorts to me. He is the most disciplined, hardworking, and dedicated man I know. He goes above and beyond the call of duty when it comes to doing things right. So to say our house was prepared for this storm would be an understatement. The hurricane shutters were up (along with our son's, our church's, our neighbors', our friends', and anyone else in our vicinity that needed his help). We had sandbags all around the perimeter of our home as well. We had all the supplies needed to survive for at least a week without power. So in that sense, we were prepared.

The most frightening thing about this storm was the massive threat of a fifteen-foot storm surge. That is something we've never experienced in our area. The governor continued to send message after message of great concern along with the meteorologists. So we made the decision that if, and only if, we were given a mandatory evacuation, we would leave and head to higher ground because our son and his family, including our two young grandsons, would be hunkering down with us. If our grand babies were going to be in the house, we were going to make the wisest decision necessary to keep them safe.

I was standing in my neighbor's kitchen, discussing the latest track of Hurricane Irma, when the storm alert message came blaring on all our phones. Our zone B was now under mandatory evacuations. I was born and raised in Florida. I had never in my life been under a mandatory evacuation until now. When I ran to share this news with my husband, he dropped everything in his hands and said, "Let's go!"

We packed everything that could fit in our vehicle and met up with our son and his young family and headed north. Our newly married daughter had invited us to stay with her at her in-laws' house, which is about two and a half hours northeast of where we live. The eye of the storm was definitely not heading directly that way.

To my surprise, when we arrived at the house of my daughter's in-laws, I realized it was a two-story wood-frame house without hurricane shutters. Then again, they did not need hurricane shutters on per se since the storm was not headed in their direction. In that case, I was not to worry because the eye of the storm was headed in another direction.

It was a beautiful home built in 1904 that had withstood quite a few big storms. However, later that night when news came that Hurricane Irma had surprisingly decided to make a northeastern turn and was heading right our way, I was not finding any consolation in the history of that house.

To say that that was one of the scariest nights of my entire family's lives would be a grave understatement. There were several of us attempting to sleep on comforters in the living room. The terror of the winds began to blow around 10:30 p.m., and lasted for six very dreadful hours, until around four thirty in the morning. Irma was an intense, fierce storm indeed! There were many times I was convinced the house would be taken down by the winds. The noise from the trees breaking with branches flying and hitting the windows, debris swirling as the wind continued howling was more than I could handle. But God! He had taught me how to take every thought captive. He had taught me that there is power in prayer. He had taught me how to use his word—no matter the depth of my fear—to conquer that very fear. He had met me time after time when I would worship my way through a storm, and this night would be no different.

God not only saw me and my family through that sleepless night, he continued to calm me as every anxious thought crept in. Every time fear would begin to grip me beyond what I thought I could withstand, I had to live out all the things I knew to be true about my God. As my heart would begin to race, when fear and terror were the only emotions I was feeling, as anxiety would start to set in, I had only one thing I knew to do. I would literally cry out His name, "Jesus! Jesus! Jesus!" Just like I learned all those years ago, I would cry out His word: When I am afraid, I will put my trust in you (Psalm 58:3). When anxiety is great within me, your consolation brings me great joy (Psalm 94:19). Where does my help come from? My help comes from the Lord, the maker of heaven and earth (Psalm 121:1–2).

Then between quoting scripture and battling my fear, I would sing whatever worship song was popping up in my head, "You Make Me Brave" by Bethel. A few times I shot up off the floor and lifted my hands in the pitch-black darkness of the night. A few other times I would throw myself up and speak or sing out a little more audibly. If the winds blew loudly, then I would pray more loudly until I would feel God's peace quiet my soul and settle me down once again.

That pattern happened throughout the entire night, especially since there was no deep sleep happening. Surrounded by the ones I love the most, as crippling as that fear felt, I had a knowing that God would see us through. Hours later, once the storm finally settled in the wee hours of the morning, it dawned on me. How amazing is it that God would show off His faithfulness to me in such a tangible way once again, right as I was concluding this book through a real storm.

Interestingly enough, I had been praying for weeks how to end this book. What final words could I share that would be the cherry on top? What final words of wisdom could I bring to the table that would bring this message home?

Then I got my answer! I certainly am not saying that God sent Hurricane Irma along so I could finish my book, but as stated earlier, He is the one that causes all things to work together for the good of those who love him and are called according to his purpose (Romans 8:28 NKJ). So when I found myself right in the eye of one of the biggest storms in US history, literally shaking like a leaf, the One who calms the storms once again became my Prince of Peace.

Keep Singing

As I shared earlier in this book, whether I'm cooking or cleaning, taking a shower, putting on my makeup, driving to work, riding my bike, going on a long walk, all throughout my day, there's worship music playing or there's a song of praise on my lips. Worshipping the Lord has become a lifeline for me. And I wouldn't have it any other way! Not a day goes by where a song of praise to the Lord has not come out of me at some point. My husband often teases me that I'm always humming a son—or at least when I am in a situation that would cause me to be afraid. My God has really become my strength and my song (Psalm 118:14)! When the opportunity arises for me to stress out, be afraid, become fretful, or anxious, I've learned to keep singing my way to victory. I like to say it this way: I don't worry. I worship.

I've counseled many people over the years whose life circumstances have been awful to say the least. Without hesitation, one of the favorite pieces of wisdom I share with them is the power of worshipping their way through their storms. Quite frankly, I do not see any value in someone spending time crying out to God in desperation, then getting in their car and fueling themselves with the latest top forty songs (or whatever music genre they choose). I can only share from very personal experience what I know has made one of the greatest impacts in my life.

Looking back, I remember there were a countless number of nights that I spent shaking like a leaf. Those nights filled me with great fear, terror, and real anxiety. This is why I am beyond grateful that I persevered and learned—even though it was the hard way—to fight and overcome triumphantly with the right weapons. Without a shadow of a doubt, I know where my strength comes from. May the same be true for you.

Scriptures That Filled Me with Faith in My Fear

In peace I will lie down and sleep, for you alone, Lord, make me dwell in safety. (Psalm 4:8 NIV)

But let all who take refuge in you be glad; let them ever sing for joy. Spread your protection over them, that those who love your name may rejoice in you. (Psalm 5:11 NIV)

The Lord is my shepherd, I lack nothing. He makes me lie down in green pastures, he leads me beside quiet waters, he refreshes my soul. He guides me along the right paths for his name's sake. Even though I walk through the darkest valley, I will fear no evil, for you are with me; your rod and your staff, they comfort me. (Psalm 23:1–4 NIV)

My eyes are ever on the Lord, for only he will release my feet from the snare. Turn to me and be gracious to me, for I am lonely and afflicted. Relieve the troubles of my heart and free me from my anguish. (Psalm 25:15–17 NIV)

The Lord is my strength and my shield; my heart trusts in him, and he helps me. My heart leaps for joy, and with my song I praise him. (Psalm 28:7 NIV)

The Lord gives his people strength. The Lord blesses them with peace. (Psalm 29:11 NIV)

I waited patiently for the Lord; he turned to me and heard my cry. He lifted me out of the slimy pit, out of the mud and mire; he set my feet on a rock and gave me a firm place to stand. He put a new song in my mouth, a hymn of praise to our God. Many will see and fear the Lord and put their trust in him. (Psalm 40:1–3 NIV)

By day the Lord directs his love, at night his song is with me—a prayer to the God of my life. (Psalm 42:8 NIV)

Cast your burden on the LORD and He will sustain and uphold you; He will never allow the righteous to be shaken. (Psalm 55:22 AMP)

When I am afraid, I will put my trust in You. (Psalm 56:3 NIV)

I remembered my songs in the night. My heart meditated and my spirit asked. (Psalm 77:6 NIV)

This one was my theme verse:

When anxiety was great within me, your consolation brought joy to my soul. (Psalm 94:19 NIV)

I love the Lord, for he heard my voice; he heard my cry for mercy. Because he turned his ear to me, I will call on him as long as I live. The cords of death entangled me, the anguish of the grave came over me; I was overcome by distress and sorrow. Then I called on the name of the Lord: "Lord, save me!" The Lord is gracious and righteous; our God is full of compassion. The Lord protects the unwary; when I was brought low, he saved me. Return to your rest, my soul, for the Lord has been good to you. For you, Lord, have delivered me from death, my eyes from tears, my feet from stumbling, that I may walk before the Lord in the land of the living. (Psalm 116:1–9 NIV)

The LORD is my strength and my song;
he has given me victory. (Psalm 118:14 NLT)

It was good for me to be afflicted so that I might learn your decrees. (Psalm 119:71NIV)

The Lord your God, who is going before you, will fight for you, as he did for you in Egypt, before your very eyes, and in the desert. There you saw how the Lord your God carried you, as a father carries his child, all the way you went up until you reached this place. (Deuteronomy 1:30–31NIV)

Because of the Lord's great love, we are not consumed, for his compassions never fail. They are new every morning; great is your faithfulness. I say to myself, "The Lord is my portion; therefore, I will wait for him." The Lord is good to those whose hope is in him, to the one who seeks him... (Lamentations 3:22–25 NIV)

The Sovereign Lord is my strength; he makes my feet like the feet of a deer, he enables me to go on the heights. (Habakkuk 3:19 NIV)

Do not be anxious about anything, but in everything by prayer and petition with Thanksgiving, present your requests to God. And the peace of God, which transcends all understanding, will guard your hearts and your minds in Christ Jesus. (Philippians 4:6–7 NIV)

For God has not given us a spirit of fear, but of power, and of love and of a sound mind. (1 Timothy 5:7 NKJV)

Rejoice always, give thanks in all circumstances; for this is God's will for you in Christ Jesus. (1 Thessalonians 5:16–18 NIV)

Cast all your anxiety on him because he cares for you. (1 Peter 5:7 NIV)

About the Author

Dina Comer has been married to her husband, David, since 1988. David and Dina are the lead pastors of Christian Life Fellowship, a thriving nondenominational church in Cape Coral, Florida. Dina, formerly a court reporter in her early married days, spent over three decades effectively leading youth ministry.

Her first book, *Help! There's a Teen in My House*, was an overflow of her passion to help parents/families with proven-effective parenting principles.

Dina's ultimate desire is to be a godly example to others and to help encourage and equip people of all ages to live hope-filled lives with their God-given purpose. Her life's motto is "No compromise, no excuses, no regrets!"

9 781098 079079